The Last to Leave

Poems by
Margaret Clough

modjaji books

Published in 2014 by Modjaji Books
PO Box 385, Athlone, 7760, Cape Town, South Africa
www.modjajibooks.co.za

ISBN 978-1-920590-55-0

Cover artwork by Danielle Clough and Jay Gordon
Book and cover layout by Danielle Clough

CONTENTS

WHAT TO DO IN AUGUST

Shadows hang over the patio.
Mud covers the thin grasses.
Dank puddles lie on paths
and the rough wind
drives cold waves high
against the sand.

Higgledy in my cupboard lie
odd socks, cracked leather shoes
and knitting with dropped stitches
asking for a clean-out

In the Old Age Complex
conversations
are of migrations
to Serengeti plains
with binoculars and cameras
and to Nepalese hills
with oxygen and
an extra Yak.

WITHIN REACH

As age shortens my spine
and makes my fingers curl,
the edges of my life draw inwards.
Possessions lose their meaning.
I leave a roomy house
for a cramped cottage; soon
four walls will close me in and
all that I need will be
only an arm's reach away.

KNIVES

Queen Victoria's cutlers
would not have been amused.
Great grandfather's carving knife,
which used to be razor sharp,
honed daily on bone-handled steel,
has lost its cutting edge
and become all blotched and speckled
from lack of cleaning paste.

I have forgotten how to roast
barons of beef and legs of venison.
Can't chew anything
but chicken burgers and fish fingers.
Now in a plastic rack there sit the latest models:
breadknife, butter knife, vegetable slice, cheese cutter,
all shiny and stainless.

Those are the knives
I'm using now.

ALMA MATER REVISITED

Dust motes dance in the wide corridors.
Footsteps echo in the classrooms.
In the hop-scotch quad, faintly,
the flip flap of a phantom skipping rope.
There is a sound of whispers
and giggling behind hands

I see a girl, ill-fitting tunic over
woolly bloomers and scratchy stockings
toil, one foot behind the other
up boot-worn stairs.
Damp fingers clutch
a dog-eared copy book.

in the faded curtains
a soft breeze is sighing.

IN THE WRECK OF THE TITANIC

Each autumn, relentless as the equinoctial tides,
my grandmother made marmalade
and I would help her take the sea-green fruits
break them apart and cut them paper-thin
with wrinkling fingers, while
the bleeding segments soaked the boards with juicy spray.

Then we would sweep the bits
from off the chopping boards
into the waiting bubbling water.
Pieces of Seville orange, grapefruit, lemon
rose and sank like flotsam
in the heaving cauldron.

As the Titanic sank, the waves
swept from decks and holds
dozens of cases of clothes, motorcar parts, filter paper,
hundreds of chairs, musical instruments, gramophones
thousands of jewels, shoes and books and –
one marmalade machine,
Brave Molly's

-- she saved two lives instead.

MILLIPEDE

A millipede crept into my kitchen sink today.
I turned the tap on full and washed it down the drain.
It curled up in a tiny spiral
as it plunged to its death down the plughole.
And I felt ashamed. It was
such a small and helpless thing.

I remember millipedes in Zambia,
not at all small and helpless –
thick as truncheons,
with a mass of waving legs
like the bristles on a broom.

In Zambia everything was outsize:
mushrooms like dinner plates,
snails as big and round as pudding basins
and a dome of sky, huge and black,
brilliant with a million stars.

DUEL TO THE DEATH

(All life carried on your shoulder
invincible forerunner
D.H.Lawrence: Baby Tortoise)

Beaky-mouthed and beady-eyed,
with wrinkled necks stretched out.
two tortoises come face to face.
Serious Sumo wrestlers
they square up for the fight.

On scaly lumbering legs,
as armoured tanks meet on a battlefield,
they go for one another.
No pit bulls could attack with deadlier intent.
No knights were ever keener to outdo
their rivals in the lists.

They clash, they push, shove shells together.
Each strains to overturn the other.
The larger tortoise gets the upper hand.
The smaller, almost toppled, slides, retreats,
then turns and comes back to the fray.

Now it's the smaller one that gets
his adversary at bay.
Cornered against a jagged stone.
out-played, the bigger one's undone,
upended, lying on his back,
head scraping on the sand,
legs waggling in the air.

The female that has caused this bitter fight
is watching from a nearby tuft of grass.
She joins the victor and they toddle off
leaving the loser, helpless,
upside-down.

Here, just as on the Galapagos isles,
only the fittest tortoises
survive.

OLD SONGS

The North wind doth blow
And we shall have snow.
Well probably not snow, possibly hail.
Anyway it's very cold and windy here
outside the vestry door, in the rain.
Here am I waiting at the church,
Waiting at the church, waiting at the church.
What has happened to John the verger?
I hope he hasn't forgotten
he has to give me Sunday's collection
to take to the bank.
O how could he leave me in the lurch?
My how it does upset me.
When I have the money with me I must be careful.
I had better go via Lakeside –
safer than gangster-ridden Lavender Hill.
Lavender's blue, Lavender's green
When you are King, dilly, dilly
I shall be Queen.
Ah there comes John with the bank bag.
Now I can go.
Here I go singing low
and rather tunelessly too.
I do this all the time –
sing to myself the songs
 my father once sang to me.
Songs my father tau-u-u-ght me.
I'm told it is a symptom of senility.

AT THE AA CONFERENCE

In a darkened hall,
waiting
for the Welcome and the Annual Report.
Suddenly –
one drawn-out trumpet note and then
a tumble into the first bars of "Amazing Grace."
A soft voice, deep and pure
"… that saved a wretch like me".
The sound hangs in the air,
flutters, almost dies –
another voice joins in
and then another.
The singing oozes
across the auditorium
and swells into a flood.

The crowded gathering,
grabbed by its scruff,
is raised up off the ground and
shaken.

PARTIAL ECLIPSE

I wake in a room of pale blue light.
Outside the door the clear bright night
has washed the colour from trees and grass,
sketched shapes in charcoal on wall and path.

And when I look up it is not too soon
to see the huge and puffed-up moon,
wiping away a last black trace
of inky soot from her round white face.

ALL SOULS' NIGHT

In a mirror in the darkened room
I see a shadow behind me.
I turn, but it has moved away

The curtains rustle at the open window
A salty breeze ruffles my hair
and fingers my cheek

Beneath the sighing of the waves
I hear voices murmur
in the throbbing of the tide.

I light a candle.
A harsh breath
flutters the flame.

BLOGSPOT BLUES

I've lost my blog. Where can it be?
I think it has unfriended me.
It disappeared into the cloud
I shake my fist. I cry aloud.
I punch the keys, but all in vain.
It doesn't like my user-name.

SURPRISES ON THE INTERNET

Three exciting messages:
First: a notification –
"You have won two and a half million pounds!"
Not rands! Pounds!
In a lottery I never entered.

Immediately, of course,
I booked ticket on a Mediterranean cruise,
put in an offer for a mansion in Constantia
and splashed out on Gucci shoes,
silk dresses and designer jeans
and a down payment
on a BMW.

Then came an offer
from a man who loves my profile
and wants to get to know me better.
He is looking for a long term relationship!
(A long term relationship?
I'm seventy eight years old;
how long-term does he think
that it could be?)

Without delay I engaged a wedding planner
to arrange a ceremony at Val de Vie,
lodged a wedding present list at House and Home
and got together all my old school friends
to form an entourage in tulle and lace
to complement an Errol Arendse
embroidered bridal gown.

The third surprise: an invitation
for an eightieth birthday tea,
starting in the afternoon and ending fairly early.

I believe this one was actually
meant for me.

BIRDING COURSE

I discover a new language,
full of chirps and warbles,
and learn to read signs of
claw size, beak shape,
length of leg and curve
of wing in flight.

Through binocular glass
I pass into another world,
see the heron playing 'statues,'
the kingfisher's helicopter hover
and the croquet-hoop necks
and mallet heads of
flamingos at the vlei.

A POEM ON THE RADIO

'I was so excited,'
my neighbour said,
'to hear your poem read on the radio.
I can't remember the title but I think
it was something about old age.
or maybe it was about death
or it could have been
about flamingos.'

THE REVERSE FLOW PIVOT

(at the dog training session)

With your dog at your side approach the four-jump obstacle
called the twimble
(or is it the kimble or the thrimble?)
Why is your dog on your right?
The kwimble(or the thimble or the trimble) is on your left.
Put your dog on the **other** side.
That's right!
Now with your dog on your left,
send your dog over the first jump.
Use your left hand.
Listen to me!
Your left hand, your left hand!
Always use the hand nearest the dog.
Step forward and pivot.
Don't move; just pivot.
Turn your shoulders; don't jump about.
Bring your dog towards you.
Don't hold your arms out like a pair of railway lines.
Use your right hand only.
Put your left hand down at your side.
At your side, not waving in front of you.
Now pivot back and bring your dog in front of you with your
left hand
Listen to me!
In front of you not behind you.
Don't spin like a top. Pivot! Pivot!
Send the dog over the next jump
With your left hand! With your left hand!
Over the next jump not the next but one!
He has to do all four jumps in turn.
not leave out every other jump.
Call him back and do it again.
Oh no! He's doing a doughnut.

He's spinning round his tail.
Start again from the beginning.
Left hand, right foot, right hand, left foot
Pivot. Cha cha cha.
That's how you do the
Reverse Flow Pivot
at a threadle(or a treadle or a dreadle)

MY LAST POEM

Some years ago, at the Knysna festival,
my legs seized up half way through the
half marathon.
"Quite common at your age"
said the ambulance man.

It was my last road race.

Recently, at a dog agility competition,
(twenty-two obstacles, and a winding course)
I came to a puffing standstill
at obstacle fifteen.
My dog ran round me, barking to urge me on

It was my last agility trial.

On an outing with my walking group
when I dropped behind once again
the leader said,
"Do you want us to stop and wait for you
every time?"

It was my last beach walk.

One day as I am writing,
my fingers will stiffen and lose their grip,
Inspiration will fail me
and as I stagger to the end,
I will lose the beginning.

It will be my last poem.

FOR ROBERT HERRICK

We do not have to rush to gather roses
We can leave their buds to open on the vine.
Even let their petals droop and fade
And fall down to the earth like drops of wine.
We can watch leaves change to gold and brittle-brown
And fruit swell up and ripen on the bough.
We've time to do all this, these days,
Because we're young for so much longer now.

TWENTY-FIRST CENTURY

In earlier times
old women had to act their age,
wear skirts long,
fingernails short
and sit at home and knit.

Now the era has come of age
eyebrows are not even raised
when grandmothers climb Kilimanjaro,
appear in miniskirts and
wear studs in their noses.

TATTOOS

When I was young
piercing was for earlobes.
and only sailors had tattoos.
Now,
rings hang from nose and navel and
stories are pricked out on skin.
Blue and pink angels, birds and flowers
peep out from low-cut dresses.
Legs blue from manly thigh to foot
witness to hours of macho stoicism.
Images once confined to canvas
are carried through streets
on backs and shoulders.

I can't help wondering
if one day,
a patterned epidermis
will show its owner's age as surely
as greying hair and sagging belly.
And whether experts
when they view
vintage examples of this art,
will recognise a certain style and say,
"That one looks late nineties to me
or perhaps it might be early
twenty first century."

LAMENT OF AN AGED AUTHOR

What a pity I don't know how
to write erotica!
I might have won a prize.
I might have been offered a
contract for twenty new novels,
or asked to be the keynote speaker
at a Woman's Awareness symposium.
I might have been featured in Time magazine
or published in Playboy.

What a pity my memory is fading.
and I am unable to recall
what must surely have been many
exciting sensuous experiences.

But I **have** remembered that
my borrowed copy
of Fifty Shades of Gray is overdue.
I shall have to go at once and
return it to the library.

MEETING MY RWANDAN FRIEND IN THE LIBRARY

"I read your poems often," she says.
"Carry them in my bag wherever I go."
And I'm humbled by the thought
of my light words
gathering weight as they are trawled
through the cold winter wet,
from township shack to workplace,
in crowded taxi or in
clattering train.
And then lifted from the page
to float about between
the noise of traffic and
the foreign voices.

AFTERNOON AT THE BEACH

The tide is low;
waves stretch the water thin,
spread it to a wide blue mirror.
On its wetness I see, upside-down,
the image of
a patient fisherman,
casting a hopeful line.

I look for my reflection, but I only see
my shadow, long and shapeless,
snaking in front of me until
it slithers under
the retreating waves.

I want to take this mirror,
lift up its blueness
and stick it on my bathroom wall.
I want to keep hold of
my shadow.

ANSWER TO DAVID YEZZI[1]

Driving on the freeway, I saw today
a pair of pelicans on the edge of the vlei
and the body of a gangster, shot in the head.
I started a gentle nature poem,
but remembered what Yezzi had to say,
so I chased both the pelicans away
and wrote about the bloody corpse instead.

---

[1] 'Poetry has become so docile, so domesticated, it's like a spayed housecat lolling in a warm patch of sun' complained Yezzi in an April 2013 article in *The New Criterion* entitled 'The Bitter Fool'.

DAYS OF THE WEEK

I live in a secure walled complex,
where we have Bingo on Mondays,
Beetle drives on Tuesdays
and knit blankets on Wednesdays.

Just up the road, my char,
who comes on Thursdays,
sleeps on her bedroom floor on Fridays
and also on Saturdays.

At weekends bullets
 often fly through windows.

PRINCE GEORGE DRIVE

A sudden South-east wind
brings scents of fish and seaweed,
decorates the road with sandy brush-strokes
and makes dry leaves leap from the gutters.
They start a frantic, whirling dance
of twists and somersaults and spirals.
An empty plastic bag
slides up to join them,
swallows some air and swells.
then rises up, vaults a low wall
and vanishes among
the bushes.

LAVENDER HILL

There's not much grass in Grassy Park.
No Princess lives at Princess Vlei.
The Diep Rivier is a shallow stream.
So you won't believe what I saw today,
Put out to dry on a window sill,
Bunches of lavender
In Lavender Hill!

CAFÉ INSOMNIA

Off the freeway,
past the coachworks
and the cemetery,
in Café Insomnia, by the sea
I sit and gaze red-eyed
as waiters glide
round dusty tables.

Half-full cups of coffee
pale and congeal
among the dregs of wine.
On the wall, between fly-blown
posters of pop stars – a clock.
Its crawling hands
drag out reluctant hours.

Reflections of dingy waves
wash over the crooked ceiling.
Stories float round my head,
lose shape,
turn into flotsam, sink
and leave small scraps
of surface slime.

Stray beams from
a blowsy moon trace
their slow path towards morning
 until,
blue as a scarab in a pharaoh's tomb,
the sky pokes through
the window shutters.

A CLOSE ENCOUNTER OF THE FISHY KIND

At a traffic light
on Prince George's Drive,
a strange man jumped into my car.

At the next traffic light
he jumped out again.

Between intersections he could have:
   assaulted me,
   hijacked my car,
   stolen my purse –

instead
   he offered me a piece of fish,
which I politely declined.

THE POLICE CONSTABLE/POET IN COURT

(Written after I met a constable who liked to write poetry)

Tell us where you saw the accused.
At a place where two roads meet, I stood
and pondered on what path my life would take.
Where exactly **were** you standing?
At the corner, your honour, of Beach road and Main Street.
And when was this?
The sun had long-since dropped behind the mountain peak
and the moon was painting a silver path across the bay.
What time exactly?
Seven forty five, your honour.
What was the accused doing?
His fingers, stretched like chicken's claws,
clutched at the concrete rim, while his scant and spidery legs,
see-sawed, and scrabbled on the smooth cement.
I beg your pardon?
He was climbing over a wall, your honour.
What did he look like?
All sinisterly draped, dark as night, with features hid in black,
concealing, fleece.
Could you repeat that?
Sorry, your honour, I meant to say he was wearing a black
tracksuit and a balaclava.
And what did you do then?
I called upon the miscreant to render to me an account.
What?
I said "You're under arrest," and hand cuffed him.

BY THE LIESBEECK RIVER

Under a subway
onto a paved and shaded path.
Green grass and nasturtiums,
a wooden bridge and
the creamy delight
of pink-edged frangipani.

A noticeboard
warns us of floods
and the danger of slipping and falling,
but we walk with dry feet
and the stream keeps
biddable between its banks.

On a radio
someone is singing in Japanese.
Choir-boy pure notes ripple
as they tell of long-ago sorrows.
and in the trees we hear
the liquid call
of a red-eyed dove.

IMPRESSIONS OF FRANCE

A country full of men in berets,
who wave their arms about rather a lot
and get emotional very easily,
especially at mealtimes.

They are passionate about food;
so French women do a lot of cooking,
but still find time to dress
exceedingly elegantly.

The towns have lots of cafes,
the countryside has vines and chateaus
and men in baggy trousers
carrying long French loaves.

POETRY THERAPY AFTER MINOR SURGERY

*(It is reported that the reading of poems is being
prescribed for certain complaints)*

It would be great if I could do
what my dog does during thunderstorms –
burrow into the linen cupboard,
hide behind extra pillows, old blankets and worn-out shoes.
and stay there.
Then I wouldn't have to tell everybody why
I have two black eyes and a huge big piece of plaster
keeping my nose in place.

I'm tired of hearing,
"O my God! What happened to you?"
I am tired of thinking up explanations,
like – I was mugged on Sunrise Beach
or a dozen pitbulls attacked me simultaneously.
I am tired of the noisy mirth,
which has been my family members' reaction
to my appearance
whenever they see me.

I am not finding the writing
of this poem therapeutic, but
perhaps someone else
reading it after a nose operation
will.

SUBURBAN BOULEVARD

The road is lined with walls.
Fierce iron gates
guard all the entrances.
Behind the walls,
people are hiding.
You can sometimes glimpse them
as the gates slide open
to allow them out at sunrise,
or let them in at night.

I also live, secure,
behind another kindly wall,
its plain facade
kept smoothly painted.
Sometimes I let a poem
creep out through the gate.

ON READING POEMS BY DONALD HALL FOR THE FIRST TIME

If I should read a new poem every day,
dig out and lift it from its printed bed.
savour its scent, hold its taste in my mouth,
caress it like a jewel in my hand
and hear it singing in my ear,
then store it in my head,
I could keep only a tiny scrap
of the great mass of gracious words
that have been written and
are being written still.
I grieve to think of what I have missed
through all the wasted years I spent
not reading poetry.

READING POETRY

A sculptor takes a chisel to a shapeless rock,
or a knife to a chunk of wood.
A poet cuts up speech.
Makes lines –
sliced up to fit
exactly what he wants to say
some lines long, some short,
some ending in a rhyme.
some not.

The trick is in the cutting.

NEW YEAR IN THE EASTERN CAPE

At dawn—
an urgent bugle call;
notes like trumpet blasts run
up the scale and down again.
It's some bird – a shrike or hornbill
making leaves shake in the ngwenya tree.
A coucal in the hedge
pours liquid music from its beak.
In the distance a car drones
early on the narrow country road.
I hear the dogs bark, look out,
to see them chase
a slithering leguaan into
the disused swimming pool.
Bees bundled in the eaves
resume their swarming.
I can smell coffee brewing, bacon frying.
Everything is up and stirring
pretending to be new.

WET WEATHER

Dad used to record the weather,
took readings every day,
(Maximum, Minimum, Wet and Dry)
squinted to get the numbers right,
reset the instruments with care.

Meticulously he measured levels
in the rain-gauge on the lawn.
"Twenty-two millimetres," he would say
the most we've had this month."

Yesterday when I fed the dog,
measuring cubes in a bowl
and setting it down outside the door,
I could tell a storm was coming.

This morning I could say:
"The heaviest fall for weeks
A full dog bowl of rain today."

WINTER INTERLUDE

Through wind, rain and hail
two daughters fly in to visit,
bringing laughter, wine and
an alpaca knee rug.

I'm told this is the worst weather
in Cape Town for decades.

But for me,
   wrapped up in joy,
   drenched in love,
it's sparkling
Summer.

DRIVING WITH DAUGHTERS

Mother, Mother, look out!
the car in front –
it's going to turn suddenly.
Slow down. Slow down.
No. it's OK. It's not turning after all.
But you didn't see it. did you?
Did you think she saw it?
No Of course she didn't

Mother! The robot! It's red! It's red!
I thought you weren't going to stop.
Did you think she was going to stop?
No I didn't think she was going to stop either.
She never looks as though she is going to stop.
No she never does.
OK. It's green now. You can go, Mother.
Well I wasn't sure you had noticed.

Mother, shouldn't you be in the other lane?
Don't you have to turn right?
Don't confuse her. She'll forget where she is going.
But do you think she really knows the way?
Where are the directions?
Why didn't you write them down, Mother?
You thought you would remember them.
What made you think that?

I am sure we're on the wrong road.
Let me google the address.
I can't read it.
Let me try.
No I can't read it either.
All right, now I've got it.
Stop Mother, Stop!
You should have turned left at the last intersection.

What's the matter, Mother?
Why are you turning off the ignition
and getting out of the car.
Was it something we said?

A visit to New Zealand after the quakes of 2010/2011

1. Passports

My fingers have lost hold
on their identity.
Their grip has loosened
and their patterns have become less clear.
Ridges once firm – loops, arches, whorls
are undermined, worn out
and smoothed with toil.
Their individuality has blurred
and now no longer corresponds
to what was stored on file.

And as I scrabble among
exhumed memories,
I lift impressions from
the things I've touched and try
to find what I can recognize
as saying –
This is me.

2. Travelling

Winding widdershins
across the sky, I sit
squashed like a larva bee
wriggling disconsolately
in tight confining cell.
My chest aches as
I breathe in the noisy
exhalations of
four hundred sleeping strangers.
Jet engines shudder in my gut.
My mind lets go of me
and drifts away
and bobs among the clouds.

3. Directions to my daughter's house

Turn right by the broken water main
just after the row of Portaloos
where you can see a woman shovelling mud out of her front
door.
Skirt the crack in the middle of the road.
Pass three empty houses
all tilted at drunken angles.
At the top of the hill where
a vintage car sits trapped in a collapsed garage,
there are four houses still more or less intact.
The third one is hers.

4. Richter Scale

Did you feel that?
I don't think it was more than a three point five,
but the one that shakes us out of bed in the morning
(the alarm clock shock we call it)
that one is a four at least.
The one that got Gran hiding under the table
was a five point five.
And now –
this one that has sent us running out of the door
and is making the house dance
and the ground sway.
This one must be a six.

5. Bookcases

After the last bad tremor
or shake
or aftershock
(whatever the media called it this time)
all the books fell out.
There they lie,
scattered on the floor,
waiting
for someone to have enough faith
to put them back on shelves
again.

TWENTY-FIRST CENTURY BOOKCASES

On the top shelf of her bookcase
my neighbour has arranged
her collection of exotic matchboxes.
On other shelves stand
a china pig, two carved impala and
three brass monkeys.

My grandson uses his
for sporting trophies and
photos of his daughter.

My granddaughter piles hers
with photographic knick knacks:
cameras, flashbulbs, lenses.

These days they are called
sets of shelves.

THE LAST VISIT

("This is how Death would summon Everyman"
Seamus Heaney: A call.)

"They want me to go to a Home," she says
"Where I will be looked after."

She puts a plate on the table.
Her hands, veined like autumn leaves,
hover over the tea cups.

"But what will I do with myself all day?"

She shuffles out to fetch the tea,
her body twisted sideways,
a frail tree bent by a South-East wind.

"I'm going to check out the place next week"

She offers biscuits, new-baked crisp,
looks round her doll-house flat,
straightens an ornament, plumps a cushion.

"I must get used to the idea.
Start sorting out my things and packing."

She lifts the old cat, lean with age,
briefly strokes her sleek, striped head
and puts her in her basket.

"Sophie would have to go to a new home too".

Then at the door –
"No, I think I'm going to stay put.
Not leave here after all."

ONE MORNING

*"On this unimportant morning
something goes singing"*
Lawrence Durrell: *This unimportant morning.*

A morning just like any morning
The sun's rays touch the slanting cliffs
at the appointed time and right on cue
birds start up their chatter.
No red letter in the calendar
marks off this day from any other.
There was no announcement
in the press, no message in the mail.

But after weeks of grieving,
somehow, on this morning,
sorrow has slipped away
and I wake to the sound of singing.

TREADING ON GRAVES

1.

The sun is shining, there is no wind,
but I feel a sudden chill –
ghostly fingers at my back –
a sickly tremor.
My skin ripples.
There is a sound of distant sighing.
The dust of crumbling writings
powders my hands.
In the midst of plans
for holidays and travel,
dreams of cruises, ideas
for birthday treats, comes
the numbering of days.

Whose feet are treading on the place
where my bones are soon to lie?

2.

In the churchyard,
after the Sunday lesson,
between marble angels and granite crosses,
the children play cricket
using headstones for wickets.
Now when I feel a shiver up my spine
I hear the thump of bat on ball
and the pounding of sandaled feet,
galloping over
my ashes.

FUNERAL ADDRESS

I would have liked March lilies,
but they are out of season.
(Remember how we used to look for them
Along the Alphen trail?)
with white wild rosemary for remembrance.
Chocolate scented bietou and pale blue sage
hold memories too.
Still – a bunch of arums,
drooping and with browning edges,
will have to do.

I would have liked a string quartet,
shrill violins and a soft warm viola with
a fat round-bellied cello or
players with nimble fingers
plucking at the strings of
close-cradled fine guitars
but I must settle for a
heavily wheezing old
harmonium

I would have liked to welcome you,
to greet you at the door and walk
you to your seats,
chatting to each of you,
"How good of you to come.
How are you? What
are you doing now?"
Yes, I would have liked that.
But – I am afraid
I have been unavoidably
called away.

THE LAST TO LEAVE

I don't know why it is
that I'm still here,
paper hat crooked on my head
clutching a nearly empty glass,
among the crumpled paper serviettes,
the stale peanuts and potato crisps,
the puddles of spilt wine.

The guests of honour all left long ago,
There were all the usual expressions of regret,
"Do you really have to go so soon?
Couldn't you stay a little longer?"
Even those who arrived late,
to disapproving frowns
and clicking tongues,
have not stayed here as long as I.

I should have gone earlier,
I know.
There are lots of ways
to say goodbye.
Or so I'm told.

ACKNOWLEGEMENTS

I would like to express my grateful thanks to:

Finuala Dowling, most kind and patient of mentors, for inspiration, encouragement and support and for her help in the compilation of this collection.

Gus Ferguson for his invaluable, insightful help in the editing and selection of the poems.

Some of the poems were first published in the Poetry journal *Carapace* and in the online journal *Aerodrome*.

Other Poetry titles by Modjaji Books